the thing
about

Mothers

the thing
— *about* —

Mothers

*365 Days of Inspiration for
Mothers of All Ages*

BLUE SPARROW BOOKS
North Palm Beach, Florida

BLUE
sparrow

The quotes in this book have been drawn from dozens
of sources. They are assumed to be accurate as quoted in
their previously published forms. Although every effort
has been made to verify the quotes and sources, the
Publisher cannot guarantee their perfect accuracy.

For more information, visit:
www.BlueSparrowBooks.org
www.MatthewKelly.com

ISBN: 978-1-63582-180-2 (hardcover)
ISBN: 978-1-63582-181-9 (e-book)

Design by Ashley Wirfel
Interior by Kara Ebert

10   9   8   7   6   5   4   3   2   1

FIRST EDITION

Printed in the United States of America

GOD could not be

everywhere,

so he created

Mothers.

Introduction

There is a beautiful and mysterious passage in the Talmud that I have always found inspiring. It says, "Every blade of grass has an angel that bends over it and whispers, 'Grow, grow.'" Each time I read these words, I think of the gift and burden of motherhood: Every human has a mother that bends over her and whispers, grow, grow.

There is no substitute for encouragement in a person's life. As a mother, you spend your days and weeks, months and years encouraging others. But let us not forget that you need a little encouragement and reassurance yourself from time to time.

Albert Einstein wrote, "Everybody is a genius. But if you judge a fish by its ability to climb a tree, it will live its whole life believing that it is stupid." The question I have for you is, "What is your genius?"

You may be thinking quietly to yourself that you don't have a genius. You may be tempted to doubt the idea and think that I am talking only about the extraordinary people. But no, everybody is a genius, and that includes you.

Who are the extraordinary people, anyway? Are they the only ones who possess genius? Surely we cannot count only those who achieve world acclaim and success.

If genius belongs only to those who invent things that change the whole course of human history, create masterpieces that draw crowds to art galleries for centuries, imagine symphonies that live on in our hearts forever, or become great presidents of great nations or great CEOs of great corporations— if we count only people who receive enormous public attention for going to heroic lengths to serve humanity—then what is to become of the rest of us?

Think of it from another point of view.

Nobody will ever write a book about my mother. My mother hasn't invented anything that will change the course of human history, she is not the creator of artistic or musical masterpieces, and she is not the great president of a great nation or corporation.

But my mother is a genius.

I have seven brothers, but I never felt as though I was being treated as just part of the crowd. Both my mother and my father had a phenomenal ability to draw the best out of each of my brothers and me. Their love and encouragement gave me the courage to go out into the world and follow my star.

But, no, there will be no books about my mother. By the world's standards, some may consider her insignificant. But do you know what the beautiful thing is? My mother couldn't care less what the world thinks. Most people don't know her well enough to compliment her or criticize her—and she knows that. My mother couldn't care less what just about anyone thinks. Why? Because she knows who she is, she knows why she is here, she knows what matters most, and she knows that what most people spend most of their lives worrying about doesn't matter at all. She has no illusions about trying to be someone she is not. My mother discovered her genius, pursued her genius, exercised her genius, and celebrated her genius. And if you and I can get even the tiniest taste of that peace—the peace that comes from knowing that who we are, where we are, and what we are doing makes sense regardless of the outcome or other people's opinions—then we too will be living in our genius.

Being a genius isn't about doing something, inventing something, or discovering something. It's about becoming the person God created you to be.

But we spend most of our lives judging ourselves by all the wrong criteria.

The world is constantly trying to make mothers feel inadequate. The world is constantly telling you that you have to do more because you are not enough. But these are lies. Motherhood is one of the purest expressions of God's genius. The genius of motherhood is both powerful and mysterious.

You are exactly the mother your child needs.

Anytime you feel inadequate, ask yourself: Is this coming from God? Because you will soon discover that it never is. And anything that is not of God should be uprooted.

There will be critics. Ignore them. They don't know you well enough to praise you or criticize you. When we are at our best, we live our lives for an audience of one: God.

Embrace your genius . . . as a mother . . . as a woman . . . as a person . . . as a child of God. And remember, all great things can only be achieved with a light heart. Motherhood ranks high among the greatest of things, so ask God to bless you with a light heart and a joyful spirit as you carry the gift and the burden of motherhood.

So, whether your children are young or old, I hope these words help you to rediscover and cherish your motherhood. Whether your children live on the same street or on the other side of the world, may you allow motherhood to continue to transform you each day into a-better-version-of-yourself. May you look at each act of motherhood as a holy moment and allow it to transform you in some way. May you wake up every day believing the tragic and insufficient stories are being thrown at you by a lost and broken world. And may you believe in your God-given genius, cherish it, exercise it, celebrate it, and share it. This is my prayer for you.

Mothers and grandmothers often ask me what type of world I think their children will grow up to inhabit. It has been the question of parents and grandparents of every age.

This is what I tell them... Tell me about the mothers of today and the mothers of tomorrow, and I will tell you about the future. Tell me about what mother's value and the values they yearn to pass onto their children, and I will tell you about the future.

The future passes by way of motherhood. It was always thus, and always thus will be. The role of mothers in history is unquestionable and unchanging. There is no substitute for a mother, in a person's life or in the future of humanity.

MATTHEW KELLY

January 1

Who ran to help me when I fell, or kissed the place to make it well? My Mother.

Ann Taylor

January 2

Let go of your plans. The first hour of your morning belongs to God. Tackle the day's work that he charges you with, and he will give you the power to accomplish it.

Edith Stein

January 3

Nothing gives me greater joy than to hear that my children are walking in the truth.

3 John 1:4

January 4

To describe my mother would be to write about a hurricane in its perfect power. Or the climbing, falling colors of a rainbow.

Maya Angelou

January 5

To me, being a mother is the greatest job in the world. Helping my girls through all the things life throws them, while also lifting them up so they can reach for the stars and grab one! That's what being a mom is all about—always being there—the shoulder to cry on, the cheerleader to never give up, the one that gives the standing ovation, the familiar hand to hold.

Bobbie Rhoads

January 6

Today I will love fiercely, laugh freely and live courageously. I can never get today back.

Lauren Tamm

January 7

There is enough time in the day to accomplish everything God wants me to do. If I am harried, it is because I am doing things that God has not asked of me.

Lisa Brenninkmeyer

January 8

It's a funny thing, but imaginary troubles are harder to bear than actual ones.

Dorothea Dix

January 9

Live in the moment and make it so beautiful that it will be worth remembering.

Fanny Crosby

January 10

Most mothers in today's culture think they are supposed to be busy doing so much for their children....What babies need more than anything is a present and self-aware mother who is gentle with herself and grounded. This grounded presence is what helps wire a baby's brain for the rest of their life.

Colleen Crowley

January 11

No one in your life will ever love you as
your mother does. There is no love as pure,
unconditional and strong as a mother's love. And I
will never be loved that way again.

Hope Edelman

January 12

My favorite thing about my mom is that she gave birth to me. She never makes me eat carrots without ranch. She also manages to give me a good life without spoiling me. She is awesome.

Savannah, Age 9

January 13

The greatest danger to our future is apathy.

Jane Goodall

January 14

A mother knows what her child's gone through, even if she didn't see it herself.

Pramoedya Ananta Toer

January 15

If I've learned anything as a mom with a daughter who's three, I've learned that you cannot judge the way another person is raising their kid. Everybody is just doing the best they can. It's hard to be a mom.

Maggie Gyllenhaal

January 16

You may not control all of the events that happen to you, but you can decide not to be reduced by them.

Maya Angelou

January 17

Accept help graciously.

Maxine de Costa

January 18

My late mother used to remind me to 'lighten up.' Those two words usually had the power to snap me back to reality.

Maya Kukes

January 19

She is clothed with strength and dignity, and
laughs at the days to come. She opens her mouth
in wisdom; kindly instruction is on her tongue.
She watches over the affairs of her household, and
does not eat the bread of idleness. Her children
rise up and call her blessed; her husband, too,
praises her.

Proverbs 31:25-28

January 20

The more a daughter knows the details of her
mother's life the stronger the daughter.

Anita Diamant

January 21

Of all the haunting moments of motherhood, few rank with hearing your own words come out of your daughter's mouth.

Victoria Secunda

January 22

Life is tough my darling, but so are you.

Stephanie Bennet Henry

January 23

The secret of happiness is to live moment by moment and to thank God for all that he, in his goodness, sends to us day after day.

Lisa Hendey

January 24

My mother, she is beautiful, softened at the edges
and tempered with a spine of steel. I want to grow
old and be like her.

Jodi Picoult

January 25

Say no. The better you get at turning down
requests that aren't in your child's best interest,
the fewer times you'll need to do so. You can say no
once in the supermarket when your child asks to
buy a carton of ice cream, or you can say it every
night once that carton is sitting in your freezer at
home.

David Ludwig

January 26

I hate when I'm waiting for Mom to cook dinner
and then I remember that I am the mom and I have
to cook dinner.

Anonymous

January 27

To me, being a mother means getting to see all the possibility in the world through your children's eyes, and also wanting to be the kindest and most generous version of yourself, so that your children can look up to you. On a day to day level, being a mother means being tired, sometimes grumpy and never left alone, and then, in one funny, loving or meaningful moment with your kids, realizing that it's all completely worth it. Times one million.

Cara McDonough

January 28

The most important things are hardly ever urgent.
That is why it is so important for us to identify
what the most important things are and place
them at the center of our lives.

Ralph Waldo Emerson

January 29

Having a child has been like following an old treasure map with the important paths torn away.

Heather Gudenkauf

January 30

A mother's love for her child is like nothing else in the world. It knows no law, no pity. It dares all things and crushes down remorselessly all that stands in its path.

Agatha Christie

January 31

Don't be so hard on yourself. The mom in E.T. had an alien living in her house for days and didn't notice.

Anonymous

February

February 1

Twelve years later the memories of those nights, of that sleep deprivation, still make me rock back and forth a little bit. You want to torture someone? Hand them an adorable baby they love who doesn't sleep.

Shonda Rhimes

February 2

I love being a mom. And I think what I love the most is the way it makes me think about what's important and what's not important. What to fight for and what to just be cool with. What it is that I'm teaching through example and what it is that I was taught that I don't want to teach.

Alicia Keys

February 3

If you cannot do great things, do small things in a great way.

Napoleon Hill

February 4

When you are a mother, you are never really alone in your thoughts. A mother always has to think twice, once for herself and once for her child.

Sophia Loren

February 5

Women comprehend not merely with the intellect but also with the heart.

Edith Stein

February 6

As my mom always said, 'You'd rather have smile lines than frown lines.'

Cindy Crawford

February 7

There were moments growing up where I felt beautiful, but I truly didn't feel beautiful all of the time until I became a mom. It really allowed me to realize no one is perfect.

Ayesha Curry

February 8

A mother understands what a child does not say.

Jewish proverb

February 9

I am capable of amazing things if I believe it to be true and act.

Lauren Tamm

February 10

It is easier to build strong children than to repair broken men.

Fredrick Douglas

February 11

A mother is a child's first looking glass into the world.

Richelle E. Goodrich

February 12

I didn't fully wrap my head around the fact that there would be a person at the end of it. I read endlessly about pregnancy and what to eat and what not to eat. And then I sort of prepared not at all for the actual baby.

Ellie Kemper

February 13

Motherhood changes everything.

Adriana Trigiani

February 14

Grown don't mean nothing to a mother. A child is a child. They get bigger, older, but grown? What's that supposed to mean? In my heart, it don't mean a thing.

Toni Morrison

February 15

Surrounding yourself with other moms is so important! You can turn to each other for support, encouragement, and advice.

Katrina Scott

February 16

Women know the way to rear up children (to be just). They know a simple, merry, tender knack of tying sashes, fitting baby-shoes, and stringing pretty words that make no sense. And kissing full sense into empty words.

Elizabeth Barrett Browning

February 17

And also, one is a mother in order to understand the inexplicable. One is a mother to lighten the darkness. One is a mother to shield when lightning streaks the night, when thunder shakes the earth, when mud bogs one down. One is a mother in order to love without beginning or end.

Mariama Bâ

February 18

I wonder if all mothers feel like this the moment they realize their daughters are growing up—as if it is impossible to believe that the laundry I once folded for her was doll-sized; as if I can still see her dancing in lazy pirouettes along the lip of the sandbox. Wasn't it yesterday that her hand was only as big as the sand dollar she found on the beach? That same hand, the one that's holding a boy's; wasn't it just holding mine, tugging so that I might stop and see the spider web, the milkweed pod, any of a thousand moments she wanted me to freeze? Time is an optical illusion—never quite as solid or strong as we think it is.

Jodi Picoult

February 19

Love and sacrifice are closely linked, like the sun and the light. We cannot love without suffering and we cannot suffer without love.

St. Gianna

February 20

What is a home without children? Quiet.

Henny Youngman

February 21

My mother had said to me, 'All right, you've been raised, so don't let anybody else raise you. You know the difference between right and wrong. Do right. And remember—you can always come home.'

Maya Angelou

February 22

You fight, give, pray, work, and never, ever give up even when you desperately want to quit on the 23rd mile of the marathon. Because the truth is... it was never about being the perfect mother. It was about being the mother who was exactly right for the kids standing right in front of her, loving her, wanting her, needing her.

Lauren Tamm

February 23

A parent's love is whole, no matter how many times divided.

Robert Breault

February 24

Being a mother is learning about strengths you didn't know you had.

Linda Wooten

February 25

The best way to keep children at home is to make the home atmosphere pleasant, and let the air out of the tires.

Dorothy Parker

February 26

I thought my mom's whole purpose was to be my mom. That's how she made me feel.

Natasha Gregson Wagner

February 27

Parenting Tip: Maybe don't leave *Hungry Hungry Hippos* on the floor of a dark room.

Rachel Dratch

February 28

Sometimes when you're in a dark place you think you've been buried but you've actually been planted.

Christine Caine

February 29

Mothers are like glue. Even when you can't see them, they're still holding the family together.

Susan Gale

March

March 1

When one door of happiness closes, another opens; but often we look so long at the closed door that we do not see the one which has been opened for us.

Helen Keller

March 2

My mom is a hard worker. She puts her head down and she gets it done. And she finds a way to have fun. She always says, 'Happiness is your own responsibility.' That's probably what I quote from her and live by the most.

Jennifer Garner

March 3

Everyone has inside them a piece of good news. The good news is you don't know how great you can be! How much you can love! What you can accomplish! And what your potential is.

Anne Frank

March 4

Love yourself and stay happy.
Happy mom = happy child.

Mary Carino

March 5

Pray for me because I'm trying.

Fantasia Barrino

March 6

She's a people-mechanic and always knows when I'm malfunctioning.

Jandy Nelson

March 7

I love meditating and taking some time for myself when I need it. As moms, it's easy to feel guilty about this sort of thing, but it's necessary. If I'm feeling overwhelmed, I'll take a walk or just sit in silence and reflect. Even if it's just 10 minutes, every little bit helps.

Molly Sims

March 8

If the scrapes were on the front of our knees, she would put our dirty feet in the middle of her chest to clean the wounds, and we could feel her heart beating, strong as the thud of the ground when we walked, through our soles.

Jesmyn Ward

March 9

All our dreams can come true, if we have the courage to pursue them.

Walt Disney

March 10

You should be known for the beauty that comes from within, the unfading beauty of a gentle and quiet spirit, which is so precious to God.

1 Peter 3:4

March 11

Children really brighten up a household. They never turn the lights off.

Ralph Bus

March 12

I always say if you're not yelling at your kids, you're not spending enough time with them.

Reese Witherspoon

March 13

At the end of the day, we can endure much more than we think we can.

Frida Kahlo

March 14

I finally discovered that the love I have for my children is the most powerful thing on earth. It's fierce and determined and an absolute force to be reckoned with. I would do anything for them. On a good day I know that I am far from a perfect mother, but I am all they have, and all I can do is to make sure that I expend every breath trying to do my best.

Kelly Rimmer

March 15

She never quite leaves her children at home, even when she doesn't take them along.

Margaret Culkin Banning

March 16

It's only hard at the start. But as you go along, you'll realize it's getting harder and harder and harder...

Sarrah Charisse

March 17

If you remember yourself, you will remember me. I am always a part of you. I am your mother.

Emma Michaels

March 18

I've conquered a lot of things...blood clots in my lungs—twice...knee and foot surgeries...winning Grand Slams being down match point...to name just a few, but I found out by far the hardest is figuring out a stroller!

Serena Williams

March 19

There is no influence so powerful as that of the mother.

Sara Josepha Hale

March 20

It's not what you do for your children but what you have taught them to do for themselves that will make them successful human beings.

Ann Landers

March 21

The loveliest masterpiece of the heart of God is the heart of a mother.

Saint Therese of Lisieux

March 22

Any mother could perform the jobs of several air-traffic controllers with ease.

Lisa Alther

March 23

For you formed my inward parts; you knitted me together in my mother's womb. I praise you, for I am fearfully and wonderfully made. Wonderful are your works; my soul knows it very well.

Psalm 139:13-14

March 24

Just as our bodies need food, our souls need nourishment, too.

Lisa Brenninkmeyer

March 25

Never underestimate the power of a nap.

Stephanie Sisco

March 26

I accept where I am in life and will make the most of today.

Lauren Tamm

March 27

If your kids are giving you a headache, follow the directions on the aspirin bottle, especially the part that says, keep away from children.

Susan Savannah

March 28

My mom has always said that you don't know what love is until you've had a child.

Katee Sackhoff

March 29

Start where you are. Use what you have. Do what you can.

Arthur Ashe

March 30

For a mother is the only person on earth who can divide her love among ten children and each child still have all her love.

Anonymous

March 31

Honor her for all that her hands have done, and let
her works bring her praise at the city gate.

Proverbs 31:31

April

April 1

The most difficult thing is the decision to act. The rest is merely tenacity.

Amelia Earhart

April 2

The same boiling water that softens the potato hardens the egg. It's what you're made of. Not the circumstances.

Anonymous

April 3

I have learned over the years that when one's mind is made up, this diminishes fear; knowing what must be done does away with fear.

Rosa Parks

April 4

What is more powerful than the love of a mother? Perhaps only God's hand in answering her earnest pleadings on your behalf.

Richelle E. Goodrich

April 5

A baby will make love stronger, days shorter, nights longer, bankroll smaller, home happier, clothes shabbier, the past forgotten, and the future worth living for.

Anonymous

April 6

Because even if the whole world was throwing rocks at you, if you still had your mother or father at your back, you'd be okay. Some deep-rooted part of you would know you were loved. That you deserved to be loved.

Jojo Moyes

April 7

Entrust the past to God's mercy and the future to divine providence. Our task is to live holy the present moment.

St. Gianna

April 8

She opens her mouth with wisdom, and the teaching of kindness is on her tongue.

Proverbs 31:26

April 9

My Mom told me not to take everything so seriously and to laugh often, even at myself.

Kelly Clark

April 10

My mother was like sand. The kind that warms
you on a beach when you come shivering out of
the cold water. The kind that clings to your body,
leaving its impression on your skin to remind you
where you've been and where you've come from.
The kind you keep finding in your shoes and your
pockets long after you've left the beach. She was
also like the sand that archaeologists dig through.
Layers and layers of sand that have kept dinosaur
bones together for millions of years. And as hot
and dusty and plain as that sand might be, those
archaeologists are grateful for it, because without
it to keep the bones in place, everything would
scatter. Everything would fall apart.

Clare Vanderpool

April 11

To all mothers in every circumstance, including those who struggle, I say, 'Be peaceful. Believe in God and yourself. You are doing better than you think you are.'

Jeffrey R. Holland

April 12

Having children puts the whole world into perspective. Everything else just disappears.

Kate Winslet

April 13

A mother continues to labor long after the baby is born.

Lisa Jo Baker

April 14

When you're pregnant, you can think of nothing but having your own body to yourself again, yet after having given birth you realize that the biggest part of you is now somehow external, subject to all sorts of dangers and disappearance, so you spend the rest of your life trying to figure out how to keep it close enough for comfort. That's the strange thing about being a mother: until you have a baby, you don't even realize how much you were missing one.

Jodi Picoult

April 15

The majority of my diet is made up of foods that my kid didn't finish.

Carrie Underwood

April 16

There's no way to be a perfect mother and a million ways to be a good one.

Jill Churchill

April 17

It is not until you become a mother that your judgment slowly turns to compassion and understanding.

Erma Bombeck

April 18

She taught me by example that how we live impacts how we die. She lived a life of courage, beauty, and integrity; she died in the same manner.

Laurie Buchanan

April 19

No language can express the power and beauty and heroism of a mother's love.

Edwin Chapin

April 20

I am the exact parent my child needs to blossom so
I don't need to compare myself to others.

Lauren Tamm

April 21

A mother's love is the fuel that enables a normal human being to do the impossible.

Marion C. Garretty

April 22

Being a mom has made me really tired and so happy.

Tina Fey

April 23

'I loved my mother too,' I said. 'I still do. That's the thing—it never goes away, even if the person does.'

Anna Carey

April 24

A mother's love is everything. It is what brings a child into this world. It is what molds their entire being. When a mother sees her child in danger, she is literally capable of anything. Mothers have lifted cars off of their children and destroyed entire dynasties. A mother's love is the strongest energy known to man.

Jamie McGuire

April 25

The easiest way to teach children the value of money is to borrow some from them.

Anonymous

April 26

The greater part of our happiness or misery depends on our dispositions and not our circumstances.

Martha Washington

April 27

Usually the triumph of my day is, you know, everybody making it to the potty.

Julia Roberts

April 28

Call your mother. Tell her you love her. Remember, you're the only person who knows what her heart sounds like from the inside.

Rachel Wolchin

April 29

I've yet to find another soul who believes in me with the same fervency as my mother.

Richelle E. Goodrich

April 30

Mother is one to whom you hurry when you are troubled.

Emily Dickinson

May

May 1

A mother's hug lasts long after she lets go.

Anonymous

May 2

And Mary said, 'My soul magnifies the Lord, and my spirit rejoices in God my Savior, for he has looked on the humble estate of his servant. For behold, from now on all generations will call me blessed.'

Luke 1:46-48

May 3

Smart people learn from everything and everyone, average people from their experiences, stupid people already have all the answers.

Socrates

May 4

Beloved, there is no way to measure the continuing influence of one godly mother.

Elizabeth George

May 5

The art of mothering is to teach the art of living to children.

Elaine Heffner

May 6

Never give up on a dream just because of the time it will take to accomplish it. The time will pass anyway.

Earl Nightingale

May 7

A mother's arms are more comforting than anyone else's.

Princess Diana

May 8

Why don't kids understand that their nap is not for them but for us?

Alyson Hannigan

May 9

Some people will question how you raise your child. Do your research properly and weigh all the information. Sometimes, you just need to trust your instinct.

Cris Avis

May 10

Life is not easy for any of us. What of that? We must have perseverance and above all confidence in ourselves. We must believe that we are gifted for something and that this thing must be attained.

Marie Curie

May 11

God knows that a mother needs fortitude and courage and tolerance and flexibility and patience and firmness and nearly every other brave aspect of the human soul.

Phyllis McGinley

May 12

I can and I will. Watch me.

Carrie Green

May 13

Motherhood has a very humanizing effect.
Everything gets reduced to essentials.

Meryl Streep

May 14

If you don't like something, change it. If you can't change it, change your attitude.

Maya Angelou

May 15

You can learn many things from your children.
How much patience you have, for instance.

Franklin P. Jones

May 16

Her children rise up and call her blessed; her husband also, and he praises her: 'Many women have done excellently, but you surpass them all.'

Proverbs 31:28-31

May 17

What a mother wants is to hold her babies when they're small and to be held by them once they've grown tall. It's empty arms a mother dreads.

Richelle E. Goodrich

May 18

Your most valuable parenting skill is learning to manage yourself first.

Laura Markham

May 19

While we tend to equate motherhood solely with maternity, in the Lord's language, the word 'mother' has layers of meaning....Motherhood is more than bearing children, though it is certainly that. It is the essence of who we are as women. It defines our very identity, our divine stature and nature, and the unique traits our Father gave us.

Sheri L. Dew

May 20

The possibility to love another scared me; terrified me actually. Being a free spirit, a part of me is most alive when roaming, then I became a mother and for the first time I felt my heart live outside my body and that's the moment his laughter became my medicine.

Nikki Rowe

May 21

A mother's love liberates.

Maya Angelou

May 22

Motherhood is the biggest gamble in the world. It is the glorious life force. It's huge and scary—it's an act of infinite optimism.

Gilda Radner

May 23

Everything I do serves a purpose for my family.

Lauren Tamm

May 24

The heart of a mother is a deep abyss at the bottom of which you will always find forgiveness.

Honoré de Balzac

May 25

I look at the cake in my mother's arms and think: here stands the only person in the whole world who'd go to such trouble for fractious, ungrateful me.

Sara Baume

May 26

Yesterday I was clever, so I wanted to change the world. Today I am wise, so I am changing myself.

Rumi

May 27

I have two kids, and when my oldest was first born, it was the most vulnerable feeling in the world. I remember taking him to his first doctor's appointment, and on the sheet, it said 'mother,' and I put my mom's name. I was like, 'Oh, right, I…I'm the mother!' You just feel so vulnerable.

Kathryn Hahn

May 28

Without you there would be no me. I am everything reflected in your eyes. I am everything approved by your smile. I am everything born of your guidance. I am me only because of you.

Richelle E. Goodrich

May 29

Having children is like living in a frat house...
Nobody sleeps, everything's broken and there's a
lot of throwing up.

Ray Romano

May 30

Mother is a verb. It's something you do. Not just who you are.

Dorothy Canfield Fisher

May 31

My mother always told me I wouldn't amount to anything because I procrastinate. I said, 'Just wait.'

Judy Tenuta

June

June 1

Honor your father and your mother, that your days may be long in the land that the Lord your God is giving you.

Exodus 20:12

June 2

At bedtime, have your child pick a number smaller than your current age. Then tell her about something interesting that happened to you at that age.

Dale McGowan

June 3

People who say they sleep like a baby usually don't have one.

Leo Burk

June 4

I am fooling only myself when I say that my mother exists now only in the photographs on my bulletin board or in the outline of my hand or in the armful of memories I still hold tight. She lives on beneath everything I do. Her presence influenced who I was and her absence influences who I am. Our lives are shaped as much by those who leave us as they are by those who stay. Loss is our legacy. Insight is our gift. Memory is our guide.

Hope Edelman

June 5

The woman's soul is fashioned as a shelter in which other souls may unfold.

Edith Stein

June 6

Becoming a mother makes you the mother of all children. From now on each wounded, abandoned, frightened child is yours. You live in the suffering mothers of every race and creed and weep with them. You long to comfort all who are desolate.

Charlotte Gray

June 7

As long as you keep a person down, some part of you has to be down there to hold him down, so it means you cannot soar as you otherwise might.

Marian Anderson

June 8

My daughter introduced me to myself.

Beyonce Knowles

June 9

No one is ever quite ready; everyone is always caught off guard. Parenthood chooses you. And you open your eyes, look at what you've got, say 'Oh, my gosh,' and recognize that of all the balls there ever were, this is the one you should not drop. It's not a question of choice.

Marisa de los Santos

June 10

No matter how old a mother is, she watches her middle-aged children for signs of improvement.

Florida Scott-Maxwell

June 11

What good mothers and fathers instinctively feel like doing for their babies is usually best after all.

Benjamin Spock

June 12

Mothers care in volumes of tears and earnestness of prayers and a depth of emotion others cannot fathom.

Richelle E. Goodrich

June 13

We all have a reason for living, I am blessed, mine has two eyes, a heartbeat and calls me mum.

Nikki Rowe

June 14

Don't be pushed around by the fears in your mind.
Be led by the dreams in your heart.

Roy T. Bennett

June 15

We delight in the beauty of the butterfly, but rarely admit the changes it has gone through to achieve that beauty.

Maya Angelou

June 16

I used to be embarrassed by my mom, but now I know what she is—she's a hero.

Carrie Jones

June 17

At dinner, have each child take turns saying what he enjoyed about his brother or sister that day. This helps kids look for the positives in their siblings rather than the negatives.

Lacey Dunkin

June 18

My mom always says, 'If you don't believe in something, you'll lose yourself completely.'

Hilary Duff

June 19

I forgive myself for being an imperfect parent.
Today I will let go of the guilt weighing on my
shoulders.

Lauren Tamm

June 20

Many are the women of proven worth, but you have excelled them all.

Proverbs 31:29

June 21

You can't go back and change the beginning, but you can start where you are and change the ending.

C.S. Lewis

June 22

Do what you feel in your heart to be right—for
you'll be criticized anyway.

Eleanor Roosevelt

June 23

My mom is literally a part of me. You can't say that about many people except relatives, and organ donors.

Carrie Latet

June 24

Great minds discuss ideas; average minds discuss events; small minds discuss people.

Eleanor Roosevelt

June 25

Why do you say yes to think you know you shouldn't? Ask God to empower you to say yes when you mean yes, and no when you mean no.

Matthew Kelly

June 26

My nickname is Mom, but my full name is Mom Mom Mom Mom Mom Mom Mom.

Anonymous

June 27

Optimism is the faith that leads to achievement.

Helen Keller

June 28

Who in their infinite wisdom decreed that Little League uniforms be white? Certainly not a mother.

Erma Bombeck

June 29

My favorite thing about being a mom is just what a better person it makes you on a daily basis.

Drew Barrymore

June 30

Beauty begins the moment you decide to be myself.

Coco Chanel

July

July 1

There's something that just happens to you when you have a baby, and you look at their little eyes for the first time when you're holding them…. Intuition kicks in, where you will do anything for them and you have all the tools inside of you to take care of them.

Hillary Duff

July 2

Don't limit yourself. Many people limit themselves
to what they think they can do. You can go as far as
your mind lets you. What you believe, remember,
you can achieve.

Mary Kay Ash

July 3

However motherhood comes to you, it's a miracle.

Valerie Harper

July 4

It's not going to be easy to rest in God if I'm not resting at all.

Lisa M. Hendey

July 5

The first 40 years of parenthood are always the hardest.

Anonymous

July 6

Woman's soul is present and lives more intensely in all parts of the body, and it is inwardly affected by that which happens to the body; whereas, with men, the body has more pronouncedly the character of an instrument which serves them in their work and which is accompanied by a certain detachment.

Edith Stein

July 7

Friendship with one's self is all important, because without it one can not be friends with anyone else in the world.

Eleanor Roosevelt

July 8

The phrase 'working mother' is redundant.

Jane Sellman

July 9

Once, she fell off of a ladder when I was three. She says all she was worried about was my face as I watched her fall.

Sarah Kay

July 10

'I don't think so mommy!' is what my child said after, 'Can you please pick up the popcorn you threw all over?'

Anna Faris

July 11

A mother's love is something that no one can explain—it is made of deep devotion and of sacrifice and pain. It is endless and unselfish and enduring, come what may, for nothing can destroy it or take that love away. It is patient and forgiving when all others are forsaking, and it never fails or falters even though the heart is breaking.

Helen Steiner Rice

July 12

Impossible is just an opinion.

Paulo Coelho

July 13

When you're feeling angry, you're less likely to respond to your child in a helpful way. You don't have to react instantly. Taking a brief break helps you settle down and think things through.

Eileen Kennedy-Moore

July 14

My mother had a slender, small body, but a large heart—a heart so large that everybody's joys found welcome in it, and hospitable accommodation.

Mark Twain

July 15

Loving a baby is a circular business, a kind of feedback loop. The more you give the more you get and the more you get the more you feel like giving.

Penelope Leach

July 16

My mother taught me to be happy with the way I look naturally—and saved me from a potentially tragic perm in the eighth grade.

Danielle Claro

July 17

Of all the rights of women, the greatest is to be a mother.

Lin Yutang

July 18

If you're worried about being a good mother, it means you already are one.

Anonymous

July 19

You are doing all the things you know you should. Good. Now, move to that place where spirituality goes from something we do and becomes who we are.

Matthew Kelly

July 20

Finding balance as a mother means accepting your imperfections.

Anonymous

July 21

Motherhood is more awesome than I ever thought it could be and harder than I ever would have imagined.

Sarah Williams

July 22

Leave your mark on the world by leaving behind a child who grows up to love and serve the Lord.

Elizabeth George

July 23

My mom taught me a woman's mind should be the most beautiful part of her.

Sonya Teclai

July 24

If we have the attitude that it's going to be a great day it usually is.

Catherine Pulsifier

July 25

Motherhood has relaxed me in many ways. You learn to deal with crisis. I've become a juggler, I suppose. It's all a big circus, and nobody who knows me believes I can manage, but sometimes I do.

Jane Seymour

July 26

Sleep like you're not going to sleep for the next three years. Allow people to help you. If someone offers to bring food or watch your baby so you can nap, it's most likely they've been in your shoes. Don't attempt to be Superwoman. You already are. You created and birthed a baby.

Colleen Crowley

July 27

Because I feel that, in the Heavens above
The angels, whispering to one another,
Can find, among their burning terms of love
None so devotional as that of 'Mother.'

Edgar Allen Poe

July 28

It's ok to have strengths and weaknesses as a mama. Some mamas play games, others listen well, some cook with love, and others are great encouragers. We don't have to be everything, every day to our kids. We just need to show up and love them hard.

Anonymous

July 29

Motherhood was the great equalizer for me; I started to identify with everybody.

Annie Lennox

July 30

The secret of happiness is to live moment by moment and to thank God for all that He, in His goodness, sends to us day after day.

St. Gianna

July 31

Aerodynamically, the bumblebee shouldn't be able to fly, but the bumblebee doesn't know that so it goes on flying anyway.

Mary Kay Ash

August

August 1

Children are the anchors that hold a mother to life.

Sophocles

August 2

In the end...I am the only one who can give my children a happy mother who loves life.

Janene Wolsey Baadsgaard

August 3

Most mothers are instinctive philosophers.

Harriet Beecher Stowe

August 4

The common, unchanging purpose of every relationship is to help each other become the-best-version-of-ourselves . . . In a family, it is our role to help one another celebrate this common, unchanging purpose. It is not the parents' responsibility solely; it is everyone's responsibility. Even newborn babies play a role in helping others become the-best-version-of-themselves. They do it by causing people to slow down and marvel at life.

Matthew Kelly

August 5

Rigid plans work best if you're building a skyscraper; with something as mysteriously human as giving birth, it's best, both literally and figuratively, to keep your knees bent.

Mark Sloan

August 6

When you're with your kids, that call/text/email can wait. They know when you're not paying attention.

David Fassler

August 7

Mother—that was the bank where we deposited all our hurts and worries.

T. DeWitt Talmage

August 8

Mother's love grows by giving.

Charles Lamb

August 9

I've experienced more adventure in mothering my sons that ever imaginable. Motherhood gives me an excuse to stay young forever, kicking off my shoes and letting down my hair while enjoying love beyond measure. Motherhood is: my life, my joy, my passion, my greatest achievement.

Jacalyn Stanley

August 10

It's not our job to toughen our children up to face a cruel and heartless world. It's our job to raise children who will make the world a little less cruel and heartless.

L.R. Knost

August 11

Whatever you are, be a good one.

Abraham Lincoln

August 12

As a parent we try our best to teach our children all about life, but really they are the ones teaching us what life is all about.

Anonymous

August 13

Motherhood is amazing. And then it is really hard. And then it is incredible. And then it is everything in between. So, hold onto the good, breathe through the bad, and welcome the wildest and most wonderful ride of your life.

Anonymous

August 14

I've learned that people will forget what you said,
people will forget what you did, but people will
never forget how you made them feel.

Maya Angelou

August 15

The mother's heart is the child's schoolroom.

Henry Ward Beecher

August 16

Your passion is waiting for your courage to catch up.

Isabelle Lafleche

August 17

Just as there is no warning for childbirth, there is no preparation for the sight of a first child. There should be a song for women to sing at this moment, or a prayer to recite. But perhaps there is none because there are no words strong enough to name that moment.

Anita Diamant

August 18

Being a mother can be tough, but always remember in the eyes of your child, no one does it better than you.

Anonymous

August 19

A baby is something you carry inside you for nine months, in your arms for three years and in your heart till the day you die.

Mary Mason

August 20

It's never too late to be what you might've been.

George Eliot

August 21

My mother had handed down respect for the possibilities—and the will to grasp them.

Alice Walker

August 22

Having kids—the responsibility of rearing good, kind, ethical, responsible human beings—is the biggest job anyone can embark on.

Maria Shriver

August 23

I love my mother as the trees love water and sunshine. She helps me prosper and reach great heights.

Terri Guillemets

August 24

How can it be broad to be the same thing to everyone, and narrow to be everything to someone? No; a woman's function is laborious, but because it is gigantic, not because it is minute. I will pity Mrs. Jones for the hugeness of her task; I will never pity her for its smallness.

G.K. Chesterton

August 25

If evolution really works, how come mothers only have two hands?

Milton Berle

August 26

I will let go of how I think today is supposed to go and accept how it imperfectly happens.

Lauren Tamm

August 27

We are born of love; love is our mother.

Rumi

August 28

For when a child is born the mother also is born again.

Gilbert Parker

August 29

When you seek truth, you seek God whether you know it or not.

Edith Stein

August 30

Nothing is worth more than laughter. It is strength to laugh and to abandon oneself, to be light.

Frida Kahlo

August 31

Motherhood is near to divinity. It is the highest, holiest service to be assumed by mankind.

Howard W. Hunter

September

September 1

Since you get more joy out of giving joy to others, you should put a good deal of thought into the happiness you are able to give.

Eleanor Roosevelt

September 2

And when night comes, and you look back over the day and see how fragmentary everything has been, and how much you planned that has gone undone, and all the reasons you have to be embarrassed and ashamed: just take everything exactly as it is, put it in God's hands and leave it with Him.

Edith Stein

September 3

Being a parent wasn't just about bearing a child. It was about bearing witness to its life.

Jodi Picoult

September 4

Motherhood is wonderful, but it's also hard work. It's the logistics more than anything. You discover you have reserves of energy you didn't know you had.

Deborah Mailman

September 5

Try to get outside together for at least a few minutes every single day and move under the sky. It's a chance to escape screens and sedentary activities, and establish a rain-or-shine ritual that will benefit your child for life.

Wendy Sue Swanson

September 6

Giving birth and being born brings us into the essence of creation, where the human spirit is courageous and bold and the body, a miracle of wisdom.

Harriette Hartigan

September 7

Perhaps it takes courage to raise children.

John Steinbeck

September 8

I am sure that if the mothers of various nations could meet, there would be no more wars.

E.M. Forster

September 9

In giving birth to our babies, we may find that we give birth to new possibilities within ourselves.

Myla and Jon Kabat-Zinn

September 10

Everyone you know will have advice and opinions about how you are raising your baby...However, you are the only real expert on your baby and what he or she may need. So when you are feeling like you want to ask an expert about something, first get quiet and in touch with your own sense of what might be going on with your little one and how you could best meet that need.

Colleen Crowley

September 11

I looked on child rearing not only as a work of love & duty but as a profession that was fully as interesting and challenging as any honorable profession in the world and one that demanded the best that I could bring to it.

Rose Kennedy

September 12

My mother never gave up on me. I messed up in school so much they were sending me home, but my mother sent me right back.

Denzel Washington

September 13

My mother does not own my hands, though she works hard to train them. My mother does not own my eyes, though she frequently directs their focus. My mother does not own my mind, though she yields great influence upon it. My heart, however, she owns completely, for it was hers the day I was born.

Richelle E. Goodrich

September 14

Your job isn't to be popular. Your kids may not always like you in the moment. But deep down they'll always love you for setting clear expectations.

Anonymous

September 15

Even more than the time when she gave birth, a mother feels her greatest joy when she hears others refer to her son as a wise learned one.

Thiruvalluvar

September 16

Motherhood is a choice you make every day, to put someone else's happiness and well-being ahead of your own, to teach the hard lessons, to do the right thing even when you're not sure what the right thing is…and to forgive yourself, over and over again, for doing everything wrong.

Donna Ball

September 17

You can do anything you set your mind to.

Benjamin Franklin

September 18

I am first and foremost me, but right after that, I am a mother. The best thing that I can ever be, is me. But the best gift that I will ever have, is being a mother.

C. JoyBell

September 19

When your children arrive, the best you can hope
for is that they break open everything about you.
Your mind floods with oxygen. Your heart becomes
a room with wide-open windows.

Amy Poehler

September 20

It's a mother's greatest privilege to give birth, to raise a child. But a woman's greatest honor is to look at her son with pride and know that she's helped him become a man.

Susan May Warren

September 21

Five years from this moment, how important will what I accomplished today seem? Will I be glad I responded to all of my emails with remarkable promptness? Not likely. Will I remember the day I took my daughter for a walk to nowhere in particular and watched as she assisted a pill bug back onto his legs and wished him safe travels home? Most definitely.

Anna Angenend

September 22

Don't become the butler. Your children are hardwired for competence. Get them in the habit of hanging their jacket in the closet and putting their dirty clothing in the hamper at an early age, so you don't have to.

Anonymous

September 23

If you're a mom, you're a superhero. Period.

Rosie Pope

September 24

Patience is not an ability to wait, but the ability to keep a good attitude while waiting.

Joyce Meyer

September 25

I like to think of motherhood as a great big adventure. You set off on a journey, you don't really know how to navigate things, and you don't exactly know where you're going or how you're going to get there.

Cynthia Rowley

September 26

All kids need is a little help, a little hope, and someone who believes in them.

Magic Johnson

September 27

I let my kids follow their dreams, unless I already paid the registration fee on their last dream, then they follow that for 6-8 more weeks.

Petite Bello

September 28

If you're old enough to critique what I put in your lunch, you're old enough to make it yourself.

Anonymous

September 29

My mother said to me, 'If you are a soldier, you will become a general. If you are a monk, you will become the Pope.' Instead, I was a painter, and became Picasso.

Pablo Picasso

September 30

The presence you carry as a mother is recognized by your children. As I began to trust myself more and more, the kids seemed to recognize that my calm and steady confidence couldn't be ruffled by the challenges they set before me.

Lauren Tamm

October

October 1

No one can make you feel inferior without your consent.

Eleanor Roosevelt

October 2

Don't be afraid to give up the good to go for the great.

John D. Rockefeller

October 3

You don't take a class; you're thrown into motherhood and learn from experience.

Jennie Finch

October 4

'Can he have this?' With first baby: 'Is it organic and homemade?' After second baby: 'He can have anything except narcotics and alcohol.'

Nicole Fornabaio

October 5

No role brings greater joy or blessing than being a parent.

Elizabeth George

October 6

Motherhood is so much simpler when you stop explaining yourself to others and just do what works for you and your family.

Anonymous

October 7

Each woman who lives in the light of eternity can fulfill her vocation, no matter if it is in marriage, in a religious order, or in a worldly profession.

Edith Stein

October 8

You've got to get up every morning with determination if you're going to go to bed with satisfaction.

George Lorimer

October 9

The duty of the moment is what you should be doing at any given time, in whatever place God has put you. You may not have Christ in a homeless person at your door, but you may have a little child. If you have a child, your duty of the moment may be to change a dirty diaper. So you do it. But you don't just change that diaper, you change it to the best of your ability, with great love for both God and that child....There are all kinds of good Catholic things you can do, but whatever they are, you have to realize that there is always the duty of the moment to be done. And it must be done, because the duty of the moment is the duty of God.

Catherine Doherty

October 10

Successful mothers are not the ones that have never struggled, they are the ones that never give up, despite the struggles.

Sharon Jaynes

October 11

I choose to make the rest of my life, the best of my life.

Louise Hay

October 12

You have permission to stop worrying about your checklist—doing the laundry, pumping, buying diapers—and learn to be present with your baby. Enjoy your precious moments together.

Wayne Fleisig

October 13

Mothers never retire, no matter how old her children are, she is always a Mom, always willing to encourage and help her children in any ways she can.

Catherine Pulsifer

October 14

A mother must pray persistently for her children,
if she delights in their prosperity.

Lailah Gifty Akita

October 15

If you believe it'll work out, you'll see opportunities. If you don't believe it'll work out, you'll see obstacles.

Wayne Dyer

October 16

Have your kids pitch in at home by emptying trash cans, making their bed, setting the table, and putting toys away. Helping out with the household tasks builds self-esteem because you trust them to do the job.

Martin R. Eichelberger

October 17

There is such a special sweetness in being able to participate in creation.

Pamela S. Nadav

October 18

You will never regret having too many pictures of your kids. As your baby grows, you'll stumble upon pictures of them (and you) and they will make your day. We've found that looking back on them as babies also helps to put your child's age and stage into perspective when you are going through some rough patches. These pictures will become your most valued possessions.

Colleen Crowley

October 19

Ma-ma does everything for the baby, who responds by saying Da-da first.

Mignon McLaughlin

October 20

A mother is a mother from the moment her baby is first placed in her arms until eternity. It didn't matter if her child were three, thirteen, or thirty.

Sarah Strohmeyer

October 21

My mother taught us to cook and to uphold the sacred family dinner.

Casey Tierney

October 22

A mother's happiness is like a beacon, lighting up the future but reflected also on the past in the guise of fond memories.

Honoré de Balzac

October 23

Mothers and their children are in a category all their own. There's no bond stronger in the entire world. No love so instantaneous and forgiving.

Gail Tsukiyama

October 24

My mother's menu consisted of two choices: Take it or leave it.

Buddy Hackett

October 25

A new baby is like the beginning of all things—
wonder, hope, a dream of possibilities.

Eda LeShan

October 26

We have a secret in our culture, and it's not that birth is painful. It's that women are strong.

Laura Stavoe Harm

October 27

I was thirty-three when I had my first child, so I know I had a life before children. But I can't remember what it was like! Having my children was such a life-altering experience. I was always looking for the purpose in my life and when I had my children I found it. I love being a mother. I know I am good at it. That doesn't mean I don't make my share of mistakes. I am a better person for knowing my children and I am very honored to be their mother. I wouldn't trade my best day before kids for my worst day with kids!

Kathy Radigan

October 28

In our country we call this type of mother love teng ai. My son has told me that in men's writing it is composed of two characters. The first means pain; the second means love. That is a mother's love.

Lisa See

October 29

I hope that you mothers will realize that when all is said and done, you have no more compelling responsibility, nor any laden with greater rewards, than the nurture you give your children in an environment of security, peace, companionship, love, and motivation to grow and do well.

Gordon B. Hinckley

October 30

Giving grace to yourself is never more important than when you become a mother.

Whitney Meade

October 31

Raising a kid is part joy and part guerilla warfare.

Ed Asner

November

November 1

The world doesn't need what women have, it needs what women are.

Edith Stein

November 2

Read to your child every single day. It helps build imagination and is time well spent.

Christine Hohlbaum

November 3

Pride is one of the seven deadly sins; but it cannot be the pride of a mother in her children, for that is a compound of two cardinal virtues—faith and hope.

Charles Dickens

November 4

I remember my mother's prayers and they have always followed me. They have clung to me all my life.

Abraham Lincoln

November 5

Motherhood is not for the faint-hearted. Frogs, skinned knees, and the insults of teenage girls are not meant for the wimpy.

Danielle Steel

November 6

Sometimes the only way to get over the sadness of your kids growing up is to rest in the beauty of the people they are becoming.

Anonymous

November 7

If an egg is broken by outside force, life ends. If broken by inside force, life begins. Great things always begin from inside.

Anonymous

November 8

'So I stepped away for like two seconds...'—the
beginning of every parenting horror story.

Anonymous

November 9

She is a beautiful piece of broken pottery, put back together by her own hands. And a critical world judges her cracks while missing the beauty of how she made herself whole again.

Jonathan Muncy Storm

November 10

Raising amazing children is a full-time job. If it was the only thing you had to do, you would still not have enough time to do it to the best of your abilities. Parenting, like most things in life, is about making the best of limited resources. You do the best you can with what you have where you are.

Matthew Kelly

November 11

The most important thing a father can do for his children is to love their mother.

Theodore Hesburgh

November 12

When you're talked out and tired out from endless demands, turn on some music and just shake off the day. It's hard not to smile when you're letting loose (and watching your kids dance).

Lacey Dunkin

November 13

Youth fades, love droops, the leaves of friendship fall; A mother's secret hope outlives them all.

Oliver Wendell Holmes Sr.

November 14

I'm a mama! I've got reactions and reflexes faster than any speeding bullet! Hugs and kisses more powerful than any drug! Eyes in the back of my head! The amazing ability to find stuff out to protect what I love! And the strength to carry the weight of the world on my shoulders to keep my children safe from harm!

Anonymous

November 15

As someone who daydreams and lives in my thoughts, I love being a mom because it forces me to be present and live in the moment with them. This has made me a much happier person.

Candance Patel-Taylor

November 16

Woman naturally seeks to embrace that which is living, personal, and whole. To cherish, guard, protect, nourish and advance growth is her natural, maternal yearning.

Edith Stein

November 17

Women are like tea bags. You never know how strong they are until they are in hot water.

Eleanor Roosevelt

November 18

This mothering role will teach you more about yourself than you ever expected.

Tricia Goyer

November 19

If at first you don't succeed, try doing it the way
Mom told you to in the beginning.

Anonymous

November 20

Answer the endless 'why' questions. This is easier said than done, but young kids are curious about everything in their world. If you stop responding to their queries, they may stop asking.

Raquel D'Apice

November 21

Behind every great child is a mom who's pretty sure she's screwing it all up.

Anonymous

November 22

Spending time with children is more important than spending money on children.

Kristen Miller

November 23

A mother's arms are made of tenderness and children sleep soundly in them.

Victor Hugo

November 24

My mother was the most beautiful woman I ever saw. All I am I owe to my mother. I attribute all my success in life to the moral, intellectual and physical education I received from her.

George Washington

November 25

Find your crew. Identify the people you can call when you need to vent—friends who'll give their opinion when you ask for it and keep their mouth shut when you don't, and who would drop anything to be there for you and your family (and vice versa). Love them hard and thank them often.

Lacey Dunkin

November 26

A strong woman knows she has strength enough for the journey, but a woman of strength knows it is in the journey where she will become strong.

Luke Easter

November 27

A mothers' joy begins when new life is stirring inside...when a tiny heartbeat is heard for the first time, and a playful kick reminds her that she is never alone.

Anonymous

November 28

Successful teaching is not head-to-head; it is heart-to-heart.

Tamara L. Chilver

November 29

When I was five years old, my mother always told me that happiness was the key to life. When I went to school, they asked me what I wanted to be when I grew up. I wrote down 'happy.' They told me I didn't understand the assignment, and I told them they didn't understand life.

John Lennon

November 30

I can have the worst day, come home and listen to my children discuss their days and what they learned, or overhear them giggling playing a game or watching a movie—and poof! All is right in my world!

Jen Jackson

December

December 1

There's nothing like your mother's sympathetic voice to make you want to burst into tears.

Sophie Kinsella

December 2

Coin the term BPOD (best part of day) and review it nightly. Reflecting on the good stuff is a lovely practice that fosters happiness and optimism.

Anonymous

December 3

A strong woman accepts both compliments &
criticism graciously, knowing that it takes both
sun & rain for a flower to grow.

Mandy Hale

December 4

Being a mother is not about what you gave up to have a child but what you gained from having one.

Anonymous

December 5

When I was a young boy, something that my mom always emphasized to my siblings and me is that it was never okay to just get by, be average or mediocre. She encouraged us to chase our dreams, but always keep God first in our lives.

Joseph Woodley

December 6

If I have done anything in life worth attention, I feel sure that I inherited the disposition from my mother.

Booker T. Washington

December 7

Raise your words not your voice. It is rain that grows flowers, not thunder.

Rumi

December 8

There are so many reasons why I love being a mama, but I especially love the look in their eyes when they discover something new or figure something out that they've been trying to understand for a long time. I love seeing little pieces of myself in them: my propensity to start singing made-up songs randomly, or the way they laugh. I love that I get the privilege of shaping the minds of three beautiful children and providing a wonderful example for them.

Monicha Wimbley

December 9

When bribing your child, make sure you google the price of the bribe before agreeing to buy it.

Morgan Schechter Shanahan

December 10

Insanity is hereditary; you get it from your children.

Sam Levenson

December 11

I've carried a child within my body. I've slept with them on my chest. I've kissed toes and wiped away tears. I've been vomited on, peed on, and spent sleepless nights cradling my child. But I wouldn't have it any other way. My body isn't magazine perfect but when I look in the mirror, I see a mama. And there is no greater honor, love or blessing.

Anonymous

December 12

My mom is my hero. She inspired me to dream
when I was a kid, so anytime anyone inspires you
to dream, that's gotta be your hero.

Tim McGraw

December 13

The days are long, but the years are short.

Gretchen Rubin

December 14

A godly mother loves God with all her heart, soul, mind, and strength, and teaches her children to do the same.

Elizabeth George

December 15

A mother is she who takes the place of all others,
but whose place no one else can take.

Cardinal Mermillod

December 16

If you want to bring happiness to the whole world,
go home and love your family.

Mother Teresa

December 17

I don't know what it is about food your mother makes for you, especially when it's something that anyone can make - pancakes, meat loaf, tuna salad - but it carries a certain taste of memory.

Mitch Albom

December 18

Magic is believing in yourself. If you can make that happen, you can make anything happen.

Johann Wolfgang Von Goethe

December 19

Even if I'm setting myself up for failure, I think it's worth trying to be a mother who delights in who her children are, in their knock-knock jokes and earnest questions. A mother who spends less time obsessing about what will happen, or what has happened, and more time reveling in what is. A mother who doesn't fret over failings and slights, who realizes her worries and anxieties are just thoughts, the continuous chattering and judgment of a too busy mind. A mother who doesn't worry so much about being bad or good but just recognizes that she's both, and neither. A mother who does her best, and for whom that is good enough, even if, in the end, her best turns out to be, simply, not bad.

Ayelet Waldman

December 20

You've gotta dance like there's nobody watching, love like you'll never be hurt, sing like there's nobody listening, and live like it's heaven on earth.

William W. Purkey

December 21

Sometimes the strength of motherhood is greater than natural laws.

Barbara Kingsolver

December 22

Everybody wants to save the Earth, but nobody wants to help Mom do the dishes.

P. J. O'Rourke

December 23

When your 'mom voice' is so loud even the neighbors brush their teeth and get dressed.

Nicole Fornabaio

December 24

Know your kid. Each child is a unique combination of strengths and challenges. Try to tailor your response to fit the kid in front of you.

Eileen Kennedy-Moore

December 25

Nothing is lost until your mother can't find it.

Anonymous

December 26

This is the most extraordinary thing about motherhood—finding a piece of yourself separate and apart that all the same you could not live without.

Jodi Picoult

December 27

I am, for the most part, who I am because my good
mother was who she was.

Richelle E. Goodrich

December 28

Nothing else can produce the joy or broken heart that motherhood allows. I couldn't imagine going through life without feeling that spectrum of emotion. There are wonderful days when I feel my cup runneth over. There are days that I want to run away and question every decision I have ever made. Feeling it all, good or bad, gives my life purpose. Motherhood is walking around with all of your nerve endings raw and exposed. It is the most extreme measure of being alive.

Vivienne Borne

December 29

There is nothing in the world of art like the songs mother used to sing.

Billy Sunday

December 30

Some are kissing mothers and some are scolding mothers, but it is love just the same, and most mothers kiss and scold together.

Pearl S. Buck

December 31

Life began when waking up and loving my mother's face.

George Washington

ARE YOU READY TO HAVE A **POWERFUL**

Spiritual Encounter?

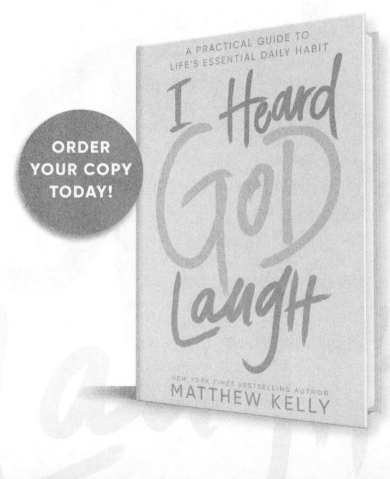

ORDER YOUR COPY TODAY!

A PRACTICAL GUIDE TO LIFE'S ESSENTIAL DAILY HABIT

I Heard GOD Laugh

NEW YORK TIMES BESTSELLING AUTHOR
MATTHEW KELLY

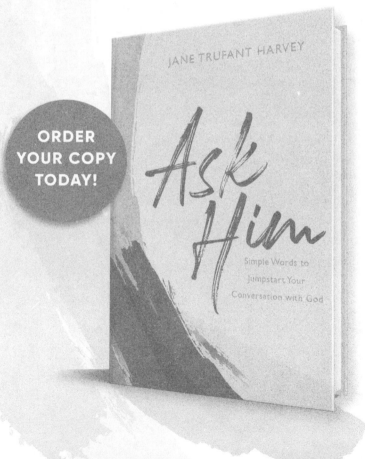

"*I am so excited for you!*

This book changed my life. If you only buy one book this year . . . get yourself a copy of *Ask Him*!"

- MATTHEW KELLY

JANE TRUFANT HARVEY

Ask Him

Simple Words to Jumpstart Your Conversation with God

Which relationship in your life
are you ready to take to
the next level?

Who you become is infinitely more important
than what you do, or what you have.

Are you ready to meet
the-best-version-of-yourself?

ORDER
YOUR COPY
TODAY!

15ᵗʰ ANNIVERSARY EDITION

The
RHYTHM
of LIFE

Living Every Day *with*
Passion & Purpose

Matthew
Kelly

THE NEW YORK TIMES BESTSELLER